363.2 Matthias, Catherine
MA
I can be a police officer

$13.27

I CAN BE A
POLICE OFFICER

By Catherine Matthias

Prepared under the direction of Robert Hillerich, Ph.D.

 CHILDRENS PRESS ™

CHICAGO

Library of Congress Cataloging in Publication Data

Matthias, Catherine.
  I can be a police officer.

  Summary: Simple text and illustrations describe some
of the duties of a police officer.
  1. Police—Juvenile literature. [1. Police]
I. Title.   II. Title: Police officer.
HV7922.M37   1984   363.2'023'73   84-12106
ISBN 0—516-01840-X

PICTURE DICTIONARY

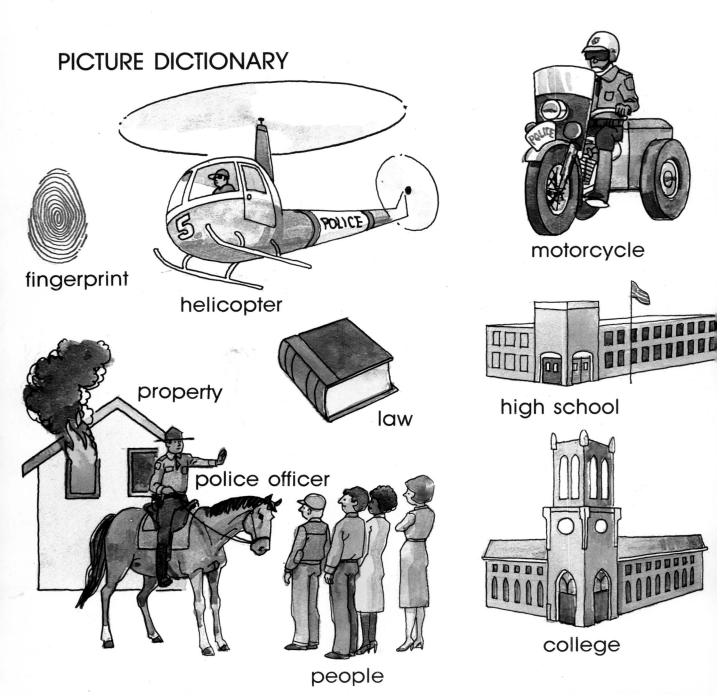

fingerprint

helicopter

motorcycle

property

law

high school

police officer

people

college

police station

computer

police radio

files

police officers

uniform detective

accident

STOP

ticket

arrest

clue

stolen property

test

stranger

drugs

alcohol (drink)

OLD ROT GUT

Police officers work
hard. They take care
of people and
property. They help
people in trouble

Police officers help people. They take care of the people and the property in their city or town.

property

police officer

people

Police officers work hard. They work during the day and during the night. Every hour of the day and night the police are working to keep people safe.

Police officers in Acapulco, Mexico (above left), San Marino, Italy (above right), and London, England (below) wear uniforms.

All countries in the
world have police. All
police try to help people
who are lost or in trouble.

police officers

All police try to stop
people from breaking
the law. All police try to
catch people after they
have broken the law.

law

The police use different kinds of
transportation to do
their work.

Beginning police officers are called "rookies." Older police officers teach rookies more about their jobs.

Some police officers ride in cars or on motorcycles. Some ride in helicopters or on boats. Others ride horses. Some go on foot.

motorcycle

helicopter

Most police officers work in teams of two or more. This way they keep each other safe.

Police officers are called when there is an accident.

When people need
help, they call the police.
If there is an accident,
the police help. If there is
a fire, the police help. If
something is stolen, the
police help find it. Can
you think of other ways
the police help people?

accident

stolen
property

Police in Chicago (above) and in Bahrain (below) direct traffic on city streets.

There are many different jobs in the police department. Some police officers work on busy streets to keep the traffic moving. They give tickets to drivers who break the law.

ticket

13

A policewoman (above) shows a young rider the hand signal for a left turn.
The policeman (below) teaches safety rules to a kindergarten class.

Some police officers
work with young people.
They give talks at schools
about how to be safe.
They tell students what
can happen if they take
drugs or drink alcohol.
They tell students what
can happen if they go
with strangers. They try to
teach young people not
to break the law.

drugs   alcohol
         (drink)

stranger

Police often work with young people.

Some police officers help young people who have broken the law. They try to keep them from doing it again. They try to help them feel better about themselves.

In big cities many police officers work only in police stations. Some answer the telephone.

Police officers in the station (left) send calls for help to police officers on the street (above).

They use police radios to send calls for help to the officers on the street. These officers go to the people who need help.

police station

computer   police radio   files

police station

17

Officers in the police lab look for clues that will help solve crimes.

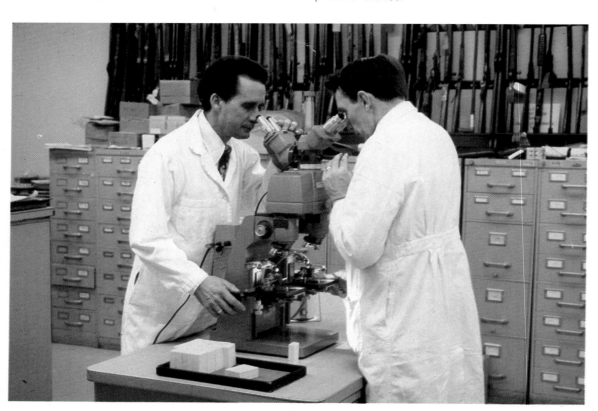

Other officers in the
police station keep track
of files and run computers.
Others work in police
science labs.

computer police radio files

Some police
departments have
special police officers
called detectives.

detective

A detective talks to reporters.

uniform

fingerprint

Detectives do not wear uniforms. They work with uniformed officers to find people who have broken the law. They look for clues and for fingerprints. They talk to people. They

ask questions. Did anyone
see the lawbreaker? Can
anyone tell the police
what he or she looked
like?

police officers

Detectives and police
officers must be able to
put all the clues together
so they can find the
lawbreaker. When they
make an arrest, they call
it "making a collar."

arrest

clue

Police officers learn to shoot in police school.

Police officers must be strong. They must be able to think and move quickly.

Police work is hard and dangerous. Police officers must be strong and in good health. They must learn how to take care of themselves. They must learn how to fight. They must learn how to shoot.

high school

college

All police officers have finished high school. Some have gone to college. They also go to police school to learn about the law and about how to help people.

Do you want to be a
police officer? If you do,
start now. You need to
study hard. You need to
keep your body strong.
You need to learn to
work well with other
people.

After you finish school
you can try to get a job
with the police. All police
departments want the
best people for the job.
First, they will give you
tests. They want to find
out how smart you are.
They want to know how
well you work with other
people. They want to
know if you are strong

test

At police school you will learn about different laws.

enough to do the hard
work a police officer
must do.

If you pass all the tests,
you can go to police
school and learn more
about the job.

Do you want to help
other people? Are you
willing to work hard? If so,
someday you might be a
police officer.

WORDS YOU SHOULD KNOW

accident (AK • sih • dent)—something that happens without being planned, often because a person is not careful. In most accidents, people are hurt or things are broken or harmed.

arrest (ah • REST)—to stop or capture a person for legal reasons

clues (KLOOZE)—things that help police officers find out who broke a law; they are usually found near the place where the law was broken

countries (KUN • treez)—the lands or nations where people live. Separate countries on our earth include the United States, Canada, Mexico, Russia, Japan, and many, many more.

detective (dih • TEK • tiv)—a police officer who does not wear a uniform and who tries to find out and prove who broke a law when no one knows for sure who is the lawbreaker

drugs (DRUHGZ)—medicines that can be good for people if taken because a doctor told them to; if taken without a doctor's orders, drugs can make someone so sick that they can kill him or her

fingerprints (FING • er • printz)—the tiny lines on the tips of the fingers. If a person touches something, his or her fingerprints often are left on that thing. Every fingerprint is different from every other fingerprint; no two people in the world have the same fingerprints.

30

law (LAW)—a rule or set of rules that people agree are good for all the members of a group or a country

police radio (RAID • ee • oh)—a thing used to send messages through the air to another radio

property (PROP • ert • ee)—anything that belongs to someone, from clothes and toys to cars and houses

test (TEHST)—a way to find out how good a person is at something

ticket (TIK • et)—a printed form, filled out by a police officer, that tells how the officer saw a driver break a law

traffic (TRAF • ik)—the number of cars, motorcycles, trucks, people, and other moving objects passing through a certain place at any time

uniform (YOO • nih • form)—the clothes worn by the members of a certain group. Police wear uniforms so that people will know they really are police officers. Soldiers, sailors, nurses, and marching-band members each wear their own special uniforms.

INDEX

ABOUT THE AUTHOR

Catherine Matthias grew up in a small town in southern New Jersey. As a child she loved swimming, bicycling, snow, and small animals. *Wind in the Willows* and *The Little House* were her favorite books.

She started writing children's stories while teaching pre-school in Philadelphia. *I Can Be a Police Officer* is her fifth Childrens Press book.

Catherine now lives with her family on the Oregon coast, where her favorite things are gardening, hiking, fog, wind, and the ocean.